I0081469

Responsibility

Analysis

Decision

Action

Result

The Blueprint Of Charismatic Leadership

www.husainmanjiyani.com

The information contained in this guide is for informational purposes only and does not replace medical, legal or professional help

Any advice given in the book is my opinion based on my own experience. You should always seek the advice of a professional before acting on something that I have published or recommended.

No part of this publication shall be reproduced, transmitted, or sold in whole or in part in any form, without the prior written consent of the author. Users of this guide are advised to do their own due diligence when it comes to making business decisions.

By reading this guide, you agree that myself and my company is not responsible for the success or failure of your business decisions relating to any information presented in this guide.

Table Of Contents

Introduction-The Million Dollar Question

Let's start by answering a simple question:

What is that one thing which has been equally distributed to all humans. I understand we would come up with the responses like air, water or some other natural resources. Well how about a person living in a desert. He always would say 'water' is a scarce resource. And a person on a hill station experiences 'air' differently than a person under water and so on.

Let me give you another clue. Its that one thing which stays with the person till he exits his life. Now you getting closer. Did you say "24 hours". Correct. "24 hours in a Day-Every Day." No matter what political party you vote for, no matter how cute is your profile picture on the social networking site, each and everyone gets 24 hours in a day. Not a second more or less. Everyone squares out on that.

Now given the same amount of time, why is that fortune and fame comes to some with a mere snap of fingers and to some it makes them go through a never ending struggle and unable to make it even closer to it. Why do some create history and some become history themselves.

As we all know history is full of achievers, the movers and shakers, who revolutionized the world in which they were living wheter it was for freedom fighting or the industrial revolution or inventions and discoveries which eased our life. History is all about action takers and though action sometimes might have been negative in nature, leading to disruption, but its still about action. What are we trying to conclude is that:

History Is Not Written
But Created

Its created by action and not by words. It's created by using the same 24 hours which is given to each one of us. That's what this book aims at-'Creating the Mark'.

Upbeating Ourselves:

What is the most we have struggled for? Or What kind of struggle has taken most of our time? The answer is Struggle to increase comforts of our lives. Don't you agree? Think about it. Striving to get a bigger house, bigger t.v., extra smart phone and so on. Pause and ask ourselves:

Are we commited to increase our Standard of Thinking just like we struggle to upscale our Standard of Living.

Today I would reply 'Yes' from your side. Probably that's the reason you picked up this book today to upgrade yourselves and and take a step towards creating history.

Moving ahead:

Growing up, did you ever look to the stars and imagined yourself amongst them? Up there in space, following the likes of Neil Armstrong and Buzz Aldrin or down on the Hollywood boulevard with the likes of Marlon Brando and Meryl Streep? Were you not dead sure then that you would be something great?

What happened to those thoughts? Why is it that we all have such fantastic dreams when we are young but as you get older, you start to shelve them away in pursuit of other responsibilities and expectations. It's not as though dreams are unattainable and impractical: after all, so many people make it big and live life large. You probably know a few of these people yourself; there's always an old classmate or an ex-colleague who ends up living the life you had always dreamed you would. What separates these people from the millions of others who seem to drudge through life?

The answer is shockingly simple:they're Leaders. Yes, you could argue with the logic that leaders also need followers; that is the way the concept exists and balances itself out. But ask yourself: do you want to be a leader or do you want to be a follower?

There is nothing wrong about being a Follower, but there is something Empowering about being a Leader

A leader doesn't always have to be someone who is defined by a set of followers. You don't have to have an army or a political party or a fan following or even a workplace team behind you to be a leader. Sometimes all that separates a leader from a follower is their attitude. It all boils down to who you choose to be and what you choose to do.

If you think it is too late to start choosing like a leader, STOP. It's exactly that attitude that is responsible for your life not shaping up to be what you had envisioned. And no, it is never too late and things are never too far-gone to turn it all around.

This e-book has been specially created for people who know they have that certain something inside them. That mysterious ingredient X, if you will. The one that inspired you to dream. It wasn't a mistake, and it hasn't been lost, it's still there: that's why you know things are meant to be different. It's why you still carry some kind of hope with you. And together, we are going to find it and bring it back to life so that this time around, you make the life you were destined to.

Remember, while this e-book will teach you how to become a leader, at the end of the day it is all about the choices you make. By picking up this guide, you've already made the first choice. Here's wishing you lots of luck and happiness on the journey to reshaping your life. Get ready to make it Big!

Part 1

Be The Jury Of Your Own Life Case

This first part of this book calls for introspection; we are going to assess your current situation, understand how and why plans don't work sometimes and then analyze the role of both internal and external factors in your life. This involves evaluating your decisions, understanding failure, appreciating the value of our thoughts and figuring out your strengths and weaknesses.

Now, you might wonder: why do you need to begin your journey by looking back. The answer is simple: to be able to move forward in life you first need to know where you are and how've you gotten here so that you can chart out where you need to go.

Sometimes, we just find comfort in blaming intangible elements because it is a lot easier to fault something that can't really argue back and prove you wrong, than to come face-to-face with the realization that you might not have as much control over your life as you would like to think.

For instance, it's easier to blame the bad weather, rather than admitting that you've gotten into a cycle of bad habits and patterns that are keeping you from committing to a routine. Or, you might keep missing deadlines because you've gotten so used to putting everything off until the last minute that now you can only ever perform under pressure and in panic. Or maybe you're always broke but instead of curtailing your spending, you blame it on a job that doesn't 'pay enough'.

So, we tell ourselves that we 'find' ourselves here in these circumstances, so far away from our goals because of the things that happened to us. Whereas the truth is that we wandered off our paths and are now lost. But it's okay. It's okay to be lost because we are now going to recalibrate and return to where you are meant to be.

And that's why we begin with an introduction and an evaluation, of both concepts and your own self. As you go along, you will see that the things you learn about leadership and the things that you learn about yourself are both equally important and come into play when you decide to take control of your life. And so, we begin by becoming Jury of our own case today.

In this section of the book, get prepared to dig deep and go hard. The point is to uncover problematic patterns, appreciate your strengths and realize the exact role and power of everything that goes into making leaders and breaking them. As they say, knowledge is power and so we are going to start out by curating all the knowledge you need to become the leader you are destined to be.

Chapter 1

Actor And Audience: Two Sides Of Your Coin

Have you ever wondered why some people seem to get everything they want in life, just the way they want it while with others, it is as though life is just another thing that happens to them? What is it that defines these people and differentiates them from each other? It is the degree of control they enjoy over their lives.

Yes, that is right. Control.

It is the Degree of Control One has which differentiates the Winners from the rest.

All of us exert varying amounts of control over our lives. Some people are more in control than others, while some people enjoy a significant amount of influence over certain aspects of their life while being completely powerless in other areas. Over the course of this book we are going to study characteristics that define leaders and separate them from other people. This particular chapter deals with the ability to maintain and sustain control.

Now, you might ask, why is control important? What does it even mean in the context of everyday life? How does it separate the winners from, well, those who don't win? The answer is simple: you can either make the life you want to live or you can take the life that happens to you. Which would you rather have? The former, right? Well, that is where control comes in: if you want things to go your way you need to be able to shape them and make them happen. If you don't sit up and start taking action, you are never going to be able to realize your dreams and plans.

This quality separates the world into two kinds of people: actors and audiences. All of us display both these sides to varying degrees from time to time. There are situations and experiences in life where you just cannot expect to have complete control, indeed, you are not even supposed to. There are lots of external factors and forces that will bring certain elements and experiences into your life and the best you can do is respond to them in a manner of your choosing. There are things that all of us go to, that we have no control over, such as the loss of loved ones, illnesses and death, professional challenges etc.

These things are inevitable. They're going to happen to you, no matter how much you might wish against them. In such situations, what separates a leader from a follower is the manner in which the person responds to these situations. A follower might just throw his or her hands up and let the situation and hardship wash over them. A leader will take stock, batten down the hatches and get ready to fight for the long haul. Simply choosing to persevere can also be a mark of strength and control in itself.

That said, when it comes to the life milestones that are open to our influence, whether or not you take charge determines who you are as a person and as a leader. We just touched upon the world being divided into actors and audiences. If you're worried that you're letting things happen to you, here are a few things you can do to take more control of your life.

1.1 Learn To Take Control

1.1.1 Start Small, Work Your Way Up

You can't make the jump from audience to actor in one fell swoop. The change can be disconcerting, and more than a little frightening. So, if you have been used to letting others call the shots all your life, you can't just sit up one day and decide to lead a multinational corporation. Yes, you might need to adopt the attitude overnight, but you also need to prepare yourself for the challenges that will come your way. So, start out small. Take baby steps. Get used to taking charge and being responsible in different areas of your life. As you get better with delivering results, your confidence will grow, even if it is something as seemingly little as planning the household meals for a week or planning a party for a loved one.

> The thrill of accomplishments of little things will provide you the adrenaline you need for the Big Race

Jump right in, by all means; just don't dive in headfirst.

1.1.2 Focus On Your Vision, Not The Stakes

Do you know what is the number one cause behind most people's reluctance to take charge and take a chance? Fear. The fear of failing and embarrassing oneself and inconveniencing others causes people to give up on their dreams and ideas much too often. How do you fight this fear when you are trying to develop a leader's personality? Here's a little trick: don't focus on the stakes, don't think about how much you stand to lose if things don't work according to plan and don't think about what could go wrong. Instead, think of why you want to do what you want to do: what is your motivation? Remind yourself of your vision every time you feel yourself floundering; it is a form of positive reinforcement because it shows you just how much you stand to gain by acting on your plans.

1.1.3 Give Up The Guilt

Guilt can really trip you up when you are trying to get used to being assertive. The first few times you stick up for something you believe in or suggest a different course of action can be terrifying. But you need to remember that just because you're looking out for yourself or your own ideas doesn't mean you're against other people! Leaders will often make choices for the good of an organization, a group or a movement and everyone will praise them afterwards, but the process of making that choice or denying others might cause a few uncomfortable moments. You can't be responsible for everyone else if you're not comfortable being responsible for yourself first.

1.1.4 Practice Control

Just like everything else in life, being proactive is also a learned habit. Remind yourself that you are strong, powerful and capable. Little reinforcements through the day can work wonders for your psyche.

Practice leads to perfection so keep at it until it becomes Natural.

Chapter 2

Why People Fail

Have you ever wondered why even your best-laid plans sometimes fail to come to fruition? Looking back, what could you have done to avoid failure? Is there ever really a guaranteed recipe for success? Let's take a look at some of the reasons why people fail- and what you can do to avoid the same!

2.1 Unscientific Planning

Yes, most plans begin as small sparks of ideas and possibilities. The most innocuous thing could take root in your mind and germinate into a fantastic idea- but an idea by itself is not enough. At least not when it comes to high-stakes situations like business, politics, entrepreneurship, law and strategic work. When there is a lot riding on an idea, the idea needs to be supported by a concrete plan. There is a time and place for improvisation, and indeed, I do recommend flexibility in this chapter itself, but as they also say, 'well begun is half done'.

What I would like you to pay close attention to here is the fact that we aren't talking about simply having a plan- we are talking about a scientific, structured plan that is properly thought out.

One of the most common reasons why people fail is because even when they do have plans in place, they haven't arrived at those plans in a manner that is conducive to success. A plan won't make the transition from paper to practicality on its own: you need to access, collate, categorize and analyze relevant information to be able to create a winning plan and plan for problems and contingencies.

A strong plan is one that is evolutionary in nature, and at the same time incorporates definite goals and steps on how to reach those goals. As a leader, scientific planning is a skill you need to master if you want to succeed in life because otherwise you're just going to be running risks all through. Never base your plans on assumptions or probabilities: get out there and get as much information as you can about the environment you'll be functioning in, about the players involved, about possible challenges and the solutions to them and so on. Collect data, tabulate statistics and come to informed inferences. Then use those inferences to devise your plan.

A lot of leaders- especially those in an organizational setting- understand planning as a must-have leadership skill. The difference between planning as a step towards a goal and planning as the goal itself might seem subtle, but it's one that a lot of people fall squarely into. Don't plan just for the sake of it. You don't need to mimic momentum and movement- you need to induce it when it's really needed. Don't waste your resources on appearing busy. Leverage them as and when they are needed- after research informs you of the same.

2.2 Limited Understanding Of The Plan Universe

The plan universe can be understood as the setting within which you intend to implement your plan. It includes the physical setting, the quantifiable elements, the intangible forces at work, all the people directly involved, the other stakeholders, the background and context *and* the potential future results. That is a lot to take in, isn't it? But that is exactly what you need to do if you want to avoid failure.

A poor understanding of the universe you plan to operate in, no, lead in, can set you up for failure even before you begin. I've already touched a little bit upon the importance of information in the previous point and we take it further here. To be able to succeed in a certain setting, you need to know everything you can about it. Right from the people you are going to work with and the people you will be competing against to the market forces that will shape you and you will, hopefully, influence in turn.

Familiarizing yourself with the universe you intend to excel in involves foresight, research, analysis and planning. It means that you need to start preparing for, taking into account and living realities that haven't even fully materialized as yet.

Study patterns, map trends, gauge other people's performances, look at people who've made it big and at the same time, learn from people who have made mistakes or experienced failure. Study, research and soak it all in. The more you know, the less likely you are to fail.

2.3 Goal Ambiguity

If there is one factor that can jeopardize your plans even before you have a chance to test them out, it is lack of clarity. You need to be able to take an idea and give it form as a concrete goal. Goal ambiguity can be severely detrimental to your success as a leader, as an individual and as part of an organization. You might be confused as to how goal ambiguity comes into play if you know what it is that you are aiming for.

Well, simply knowing what you want to achieve is not enough to constitute a realistic goal. You also need to have clear-cut answers to:

- How you intend to achieve it?

- What are the tools and strategies you will use?

- When will you achieve your goal by?

- How do you define goal achievement?

- What is the timeline you are following?

- Who are the people you will be working with?

- What are the measurement and evaluation mechanisms you'll be using?

- What contingency plans and counter-measures do you have in place?

- What are the resources you have access to?

2.4 The Wrong Team

Being a leader is all about being able to stand apart from the crowd, but you do need to be part of the right crowd if you want your plans to work. As a leader, and this is especially true when we talk about leadership in a business or political context, it is very important to put together a team that works well towards the same goals. It is important that you choose and direct one that works for the fulfillment of your goals. As a leader, the people you surround yourself with are your biggest resource. You need to pay close attention to factors like:

- Who you are going to include.

- The number of people you want board.

- The different roles you need fulfilled.

- Which person is going to essay what role.

- Each person's strengths and weaknesses.

- Overall communication.

- Team cohesiveness.

- Individual relationships and bonds.

2.5 Resistance To Change

The good thing about plans is that they can give you a head start on achieving goals, and the better you plan for a situation, the lower are the chances of something catching you off-guard. However, life is very unpredictable and I am always advocating people to expect the unexpected.

Have you heard that old adage about how 'change is the only constant'? This is a principle you really need to start appreciating if you want to make it big as a leader. As a leader, you need to be able to think on your feet. Market forces, bureaucratic norms, laws, regulations, governments- all of it can change at the drop of a hat. You need to be flexible, adaptable and strong.

Just because you've devised a fantastic plan and your team is in agreement does not mean that you should shut out new ideas if they come up during the course of action. And we have already talked about how sometimes things are beyond our control, and as a leader sometimes your only option is to play the hand you have been dealt. Some parts of your plan might not work in reality or might be obsolete in the light of a new development but this does not mean that the entire plan needs to be shelved. Tweaking the parts that do not work will keep your plan from failing. You just need to get good at adjusting.

Chapter 3

The Potential Of Attitude: Powerful or Poisonous

Have you ever wondered why some people go through life with a cloud over their heads, while others are always full of sunshine and good cheer? Which ones do you think are more likely to succeed? Yes, you could argue that a life devoid of success is what makes some people negative, but remember what we learned in Chapter 1 about the power of asserting control and being proactive? You are no longer going to let things happen to you and be the product of your circumstances: you are going to create the circumstances you want. And that begins with your attitude. In this chapter we are going to look at why attitudes are crucial to leadership and what you can do to adopt the attitude you need to be a strong leader.

3.1 The Power Of Attitudes

Your attitude shapes everything- from the choices you make to your responses and reactions to the developments in your life. Right from the beginning we've been talking about the fact that even though life's experiences, challenges and triggers are universal and shared, leaders have thoughts, approaches and decisions that are different. In other words, it is not about luck or circumstances or opportunities, because we all get our fair share of good and bad things in our lives. What we choose to do with these external elements defines us as people. And what we do is determined by our attitudes.

Attitudes are incredibly important because they can make or break you as a leader.As a leader you have a lot of responsibility and a lot of people who look up to you and count on you; with the right kind of attitude you can defeat any trial but with a negative attitude you might fall apart and let down everyone who's ever believed in you.

Attitude spells the difference- whether you believe in yourself or you believe in the problem.

Your attitude is essentially what determines whether you win or lose at life. A lot of people start out strong and are dedicated to their goal or cause, but as time passes, they get complacent and tired and let fatigue take over. Why does it happen that we go from wanting to thrive to just being content with being able to survive? Our attitudes change, that's what. You change from being a go-getter to being a let-goer. And the scary thing is that most people don't even realize that a change is taking place. Indeed, most of the people who I speak to about leadership values and the power of realizing dreams share how they can barely recognize who they've become but they don't know when they changed either. That is because our attitudes are both a subtle and a powerful aspect of our personalities: they influence everything we do but we're barely even aware of their presence.

The good thing is that since attitudes can and do change, you can transform yours to suit the new, powerful you.

3.2 Attitude Adjustments- 5 Tricks To Thinking Like A Leader

3.2.1 Be Optimistic Not Naïve; Be Careful Not Cynical

No, those aren't all the same words dressed up to look

different and confuse you. There is such a thing as being positive but not 'too positive' and being cautious but not so much that you end up pessimistic. The point is to open yourself up to opportunities and possibilities without leaving yourself vulnerable. How do you do that? Well, you prepare your best and give it all you've got and have a contingency plan in place- and then leave the rest to unfold as it will.

So, for instance, if you want to start your own business but don't come from a long line of entrepreneurial stalwarts, there is absolutely no reason that you shouldn't go ahead anyway; research, hard work, commitment and courage are all you need. Armed with a little foresight and some 'backup plans', you're good to go. Now, to get that plan off the ground you need some optimism. Some faith, if you will. But jumping right in with your eyes closed and praying on a miracle isn't advised either. The key is balance.

Look towards the best, keep an eye out for the worst and work for it all!

3.2.2 Think 'Challenge', Not 'Obstacle'

The moment you attach the label 'obstacle' to something, you subconsciously start thinking about it as something you could trip over, something that could bring you to a crashing halt. You give it the identity of something that is capable of being your undoing. But when you look at the same thing as a challenge, you start looking at it as something you can meet head-on and something you have the potential to beat. It is incredible, isn't it, what a change in words can do? Because it isn't about the words themselves: it is about the feelings they evoke and the effect they have on you. It is okay to look at a development or a person or a thing as an opponent; just don't undermine your own potential.

Here's how it works. Let's say you've got a meeting with potential investors at the end of the week that you need to prepare for and a dozen other tasks to attend to. When you're thinking about all you have to do, instead of "this schedule is impossible to achieve", reframe your thoughts to echo, "this schedule is tough but by prioritizing tasks I can prep for the meeting in time". In either case you're ultimately going to have to rearrange tasks on your to-do list, but the way in which you think *about* doing so can make all the difference to your experience.

Using positive language helps you link the end you want to the end you get: you need to tell yourself that the only resolution to a given problem is in you working your way through/ around it, and not in giving up or being otherwise defeated. Because you're better than that. You're capable.

3.2.3 Look At The Bigger Picture

Every time you find yourself thinking negatively, remind yourself of how the tiniest things can have the most far-reaching consequences. Remember the concept about the Butterfly Effect? It is an element of chaos theory that postulates that even the smallest events can go on to have tremendous impacts on seemingly unrelated things at a much later point in time. The metaphorical case study argues that the flapping wings of a butterfly can go on to affect a hurricane at a different place and time.

So, in the same way, your attitude can have an unbelievable impact on your life. You must make an effort to consciously monitor your own thoughts and internal monologues all the time. What you think today can decide what you do tomorrow and that will influence the life you have for years to come.

So, the next time you think you can't do a particular task or you think a meeting is "just not worth the effort" or you find yourself regretting taking chances, remind yourself that a year from today, you'd have wished you'd thought differently a year back!

Chapter 4

Let's Get Critical:

Self-Analysis For Self-Improvement

Have you ever wondered why your ideas about yourself never seem to match other people's appraisals of you? And they don't seem to really translate into the life you lead? This happens because sometimes there is a very big gap between who we are, who we think we are and who we want to be. You should always, always strive to achieve the last.

If you find yourself wondering what separates winners from losers and which one you are, remember: it's all up to you. You decide whether you win at life or lose. You decide whether you lead the pack or follow with the herd. You decide whether your dreams come true or they stay the stuff of nighttime musings.

But how *do* you decide all these things? By getting in touch with yourself. By understanding yourself. The mark of a leader is their ability to appraise people and gauge their strengths and weaknesses and decide how to work with them and what they need in order to realize their full potential. This seems to come almost instinctively to leaders, but the truth is that it's a skill that is honed with time. And you can begin by practicing on yourself. It's time to make the one introduction you've never bothered with!

Here are some questions to ask yourself:

- What is my vision for this enterprise/endeavor?

- What are the specific goals I want to achieve?

- Am I prepared to do whatever it takes?

- What does it take?

- What are my priorities?

- Which are essential and which are urgent?

- What are my strengths?

- What can I do to magnify these?

- What are my weaknesses?

- What can I do to overcome these?

- What can I do to contain the weaknesses I can't overcome?

- Are my ideas/ plans relevant? Will they continue to be- in five years? In ten years? In fifteen years?

- What do I want to be known for? What accolades to I want to earn? What do I hope to be remembered as?

- What were my five best decisions? What did I learn from them?

- What were five decisions I wish I hadn't taken? How would I have taken them differently?

Asking yourself these questions can divulge a wealth of information about who you are- things that you might not even know yourself. And the first step to perfecting anything is in understanding it. So, get ready to get critical!

Part 2

Taking Responsibility & Keep Analyzing

This section of the book deals with responsibility. The concept of responsibility is a very interesting one because it's so hard to pin down. Most of us understand responsibility in a very negative light- a fact that we're going to discuss later in the coming chapters.

Being responsible can mean so many different things. It could mean that you've been entrusted with a particular task or duty. It could mean that something you've done has caused a particular result. Or it could mean that you conduct yourself in a manner that is thoughtful and sensible and you do your best to fulfill the tasks assigned to you- whether by yourself, by others or by greater life circumstances.

Has that got your head spinning? Don't worry! We're going to clear it all up soon enough.

Chapter 5

The Dreaded 'R' Word

Have you ever wondered why the mere mention of responsibility makes people cringe? Why do we get so appalled at the thought of being responsible for something or someone or some task? Why is the general human attitude towards responsibility one of revulsion and fear?

Imagine this: you're sitting in a boardroom and the manager or the employer asks, "who'd like to take responsibility for..." and suddenly everyone's shuffling around and avoiding eye contact and looking at their laps. Or remember back when you were younger and in school and the teacher would ask a question and suddenly everyone would start doing the very same things? Funny how little our tactics change even as the years pass! Young or old, we're all rushing to avoid responsibility.

And that is primarily because 'responsibility' itself is understood negatively. We immediately associate it with being in trouble for something.

Yes, accepting responsibility for mistakes is a very big part of building yourself up to be a strong leader. A lot of people don't even recognize the mistakes they have made in life. Most of us see the consequences of our mistakes and chalk them up as bad luck, unfortunate circumstances or other people. To begin with, that has got to stop. Yes, there will often be elements that are outside of your control and they will exert some kind of influence on your life but you are the one who makes your life; even external factors only have as much power as you allow them to have. So, that's one of the biggest lessons to take away from this e-book.

Blaming other people or forces is much easier than accepting the truth and that is that something in your decisions took you away from your course and led you here instead. You're responsible. And you need to accept that responsibility.

However it goes far beyond owning up to and making amends for mistakes. It is about taking control of situations, accepting the charge of fulfilling expectations, being accountable for the consequences of your actions and bearing the onus of completing duties and goals to perfection. But above all else, it is the willingness to do these things voluntarily and gladly.

It is about stepping up and asking for responsibility, and not having it handed down to you or forced upon you. That's what separates a true leader from others: he or she is always willing to put their neck on the line. Where do they get the courage or the motivation to do so? It's because they know that they're going to do such a good job that they have nothing to lose. So, responsibility is about welcoming expectations because you know you are going to exceed them.

Chapter 6

Reimagining Responsibility: From 'No' to 'Now!'

Have you ever wondered how some people are always willing to shoulder responsibilities- no matter how great the stakes? Do you find them admirable and wish you were like them, but when the time comes to step up you can't seem to make yourself raise that hand or sign your name on the task sheet?

Reimagining responsibility is all in the power of the mind. Stop looking at it as 'blame' and start looking at it as 'credit'. It is as simple and as powerful as that! If you do a good job, you're not going to mind being responsible; in fact, you are going to love every minute of it.

Your experience with responsibility depends entirely upon the quality of effort that you put in. In other words, responsibility itself isn't the problem. Having to deal with the negative consequences of not fulfilling your responsibilities is what is bothersome. How do you avoid that? Not by avoiding responsibility itself- as most people would do! You tackle responsibilities by accepting them wholeheartedly and upholding your end of the bargain to the best of your ability.

You might argue that as perfect as that sounds on paper, it's the last thing you actually want to do in person. So, where does that leave you? Well, in the previous chapter we studied how the key to taking responsibilities is in welcoming them and putting your best foot forward. The first step in being able to do that is to get comfortable with the very notion of responsibility. When it's something that you have been shunning all your life or you do not have a lot of experience with, this might be the last thing you want to do. But do it you must, if you want to become a formidable leader.

6.1 Reimagining Responsibility

Here are some great tips and tricks for reshaping your attitude about responsibility:

6.1.1 Don't Run From It

The moment you start looking to avoid something, it builds up to a much more problematic and terrible notion in your head than it really is. The longer you let the apprehensions in your head build, the more they'll take root.

When you start acting like you fear something, it actually creates or magnifies a fear that may not have previously existed or been very significant. We often self-sabotage without realizing it, and this is one of the most common reasons why we aren't able to match the idea of our selves in our minds with the people we are in daily life.

The next time you know that an opportunity or position is opening up, stick around. If you're not ready to volunteer just yet, don't. Maybe it will find its way to you one way or another, maybe it won't. In either case, you've got to stop feeding your fears.

6.1.2 Avoid Absolutes

Don't look at consequences as absolutes. If you think things can only end in 'right' or 'wrong', 'good' or 'bad' and 'solved' or 'ruined', you're going to set yourself up to fail. And your mind knows that, so it's going to try to avoid the situation altogether. Instead of trying to arrive at a qualifier for a conclusion, work to actually complete the task itself. So, for example, instead of trying to 'impress the boss' you should focus on completing today's task before the end of business.

6.1.3 Be Invested, Be Interested

Most people shirk responsibilities because they are not interested in their surroundings and invested in the people around them. In most cases, especially in professional settings, the common attitude that most people possess is that of 'each man for himself'. As a result, when an occasion demanding hard work and initiative comes along, nobody wants to inconvenience themselves for the sake of others around them and the greater health of the organization.

Whether you are a leader at the very apex of the organizational pecking order or an employee at one of its many levels, you need to care about the people you work with and the goal you work for. When you stop looking out only for yourself and start looking at accomplishing targets for overall organizational success, you feel more inspired to take on and essay greater roles. A very big part of being good with responsibility is being selfless; that is why people who are responsible by nature make good leaders: they have it in them to look out for and work for the betterment of everyone, and not just themselves.

6.1.4 Don't Be Fatalistic

So many people that I speak with simply shun responsibilities because they think their actions won't matter. It's such a common trend; everyone feels that their contributions don't amount to much so why should they waste time making an effort and inviting potential criticism.

When was the last time you thought "oh it doesn't matter what I do, everything's fixed/ predetermined anyway"?

Do you know what thoughts like these do? They render us victims of our own making. Because every little thought, action and word of yours count. But when you choose to do nothing with them, you lose control of outcomes and futures. And then, when something random and unplanned shapes up you can only suffer through it, all the while thinking, "I knew no good would come out of this anyway". It is a cycle that reinforces itself, and one you must stop today.

Leaders embrace every opportunity that comes their way because it is a chance to change things, challenge the status quo, improve circumstances and create progress. Be the writer of your own happy endings.

6.2 Welcoming Responsibility

Now that you find yourself getting a little more comfortable with the idea and implications of responsibility, the next step is to learn to accept it and embrace it. Here are some things you can do to become more responsible starting today!

6.2.1 Step Up

Don't wait till someone hands you a responsibility. That will make it seem like you had no choice in the matter- a thought that's going to stick and chafe. It always feels good to be in control. So, start exerting control, even in ways you're not used to just yet. You'll find that the more you treat yourself like a leader, the more you'll feel like one.

The minute you start owning the decision, it becomes easier to act on it. We've talked about how life happens to some people, while others make it happen for themselves. You need to be a victor and not a victim, and for that, you should take the initiative to hold yourself accountable. Think of it this way: there is power in surrender, and if you do it willingly, it is not surrender at all!

6.2.2 Stop The Blame Game

It's dangerously easy to blame other people for your troubles, or the troubles around you. But once the habit sets in, it can be very difficult to shake. Blaming other people and factors is a sign of weakness because it shows that even when you're accepting responsibility on the face of it, you're not really acting on it. It means that you only want to enjoy the praise, but you aren't earning it and aren't willing to be accountable for when your actions aren't enough or give way to unplanned results.

Another, more covert, danger of blaming others is that it moves you away from reality. It's a process of justifying your own shortcomings where you rationalize your own argument to prove that you're not at fault, even if you really are. You cannot hope to be a leader if you aren't honest, accurate and consistent in your approach to everything. If 'not my fault/ not my problem' is your go-to mode, you're in big trouble!

So, starting today, stop assigning blame and start accepting responsibility. Be mindful of your thoughts and be honest with yourself: we all have that inner voice that starts to speak up when we're lying to ourselves or others and you need to listen to that the next time you're tempted to run from responsibility. Also pay close attention to the conversations you have with other people and whenever you find yourself veering towards accusing someone else, stop. Take a moment to think, rework your opinion and continue honestly.

Just like all other leadership skills, the ability to accept responsibility is also a work in progress. The secret is to keep your eyes on the prize and know that responsibility reaps rewards.

Chapter 7

Greater Responsibilities = Greater Rewards

Have you ever wondered why the people who make the big leaps always land safely on the other side, while you, who always played it safe, never seem to reach your desired destination?

Well, remember that old saying about how fortune favors the bold? It is true. People who accept responsibilities happily usually end up doing much better than those that don't. You might look at it as a risk, but those who have been in the game for a long time know that it is a gamble that almost always pays off. It's quite rational really: the greater the stakes, the better the rewards.

Now, you might wonder, doesn't all this talk of 'stakes', 'gambles' and 'risks' go against all that you have learned so far and the advice that I've given you? To be perfectly honest, both life and leadership involves taking lots of risks. You have to be prepared to go where nobody else has dared if you want to be a pioneer and a trailblazer. You can't just keep playing by the rules and walking the straight-and-narrow if you want to live a life that is large in every sense of the word. You need to be ready to up the ante every time and keep pushing forward, out of your comfort zone and beyond the limits.

Now, all this talk about risk-taking might sound counterintuitive to all that we have been talking about so far, but when you pay close attention, it all starts to come together to form one undeniable truth: leaders have courage.

If you play in the small leagues, you can never expect to win the sweepstakes. But if you are ready to accept greater responsibilities, face down bigger challenges and never quit, then you can be assured of a life that is everything you dreamed of and more.

How does responsibility fit into all this? Well, accepting responsibility is a sort of risk in

itself, isn't it? What if it doesn't go well? What if you don't perform as desired? What if you can't deliver? What if you lose what you already have chasing after something uncertain? It is because of these concerns that most people prefer to function within their boxes; what most of us don't realize is that the walls that keep us safe are also the ones that limit us.

Take a look around. In any organization, the highest-paid employees are always the ones who are takes on more responsibilites. In any industry, the top grossers are always the players that are pushing the limits and taking on more and more. It might sound exhausting, but constantly expanding, adding to your portfolio and your workload is the only way to keep growing. That's how you go from being an individual to being an asset. That is how you start earning what you deserve- by expanding the limits of what you deserve and how hard you work to get it!

So, don't worry about the risks. All successful leaders know that the gap between the stakes and the reward- that looming chasm of risks- is easily closed with hard work, determination and pure drive.

Part 3

Taking Decisions

This section of the book deals with decision-making. As a leader, in life and in business, you need to be able to take a call on different choices and options on an almost-daily basis. And it's not enough to simply be willing to make decisions: you need to be able to make good decisions that benefit you, your cause or organization and the people depending on you.

People often look at decisions as short-lived choices that they need to make in order to move on to the next moment, hour, day or choice. In reality, a decision that you take today has the potential to shape your life for decades to come.

And so, mastering the art of making decisions like a pro is something that will stand you in good stead for the rest of your life. From making money in business to choosing the best for your loved ones, decision-making is all about being able to correctly identify choices, weigh options, evaluate potential risks and gains, foresee outcomes and then come to a conclusion on the most preferred course of action.

Chapter 8

Looking Back:

Decisions That Made You Who You Are

Have you ever wondered why things make so much sense when you work backwards from the present but you remember feeling only confusion, stress and uncertainty in the original moment itself? It's because back then you had no way of knowing how things would turn out: would your plans work or would they fail? Sometimes we do well and sometimes we don't; in either case, things always seem much clearer in retrospect. We learn about how we could have fine-tuned certain good moves, or what we would avoid/undo or change if we had a chance to do things over.

We all have decisions that we can remember taking clearly. For example, most of us remember evaluating universities before zeroing in on one that had that little something extra as compared to all our backup schools. Or you might remember a certain relationship you walked away from in order to allow yourself to grow. Or maybe a job that you regret passing up on because back then it just didn't pay enough and you needed the money, even though you knew it would make for a great learning experience. These are the decisions that our memory holds onto because they contribute in a very noticeable way to who we are, what we become and where we end up in life.

There are often other decisions as well that are less obvious in their being but are just as impactful. If you were to look back on your life right now and think of all the big and little choices you made, you'll see that every single one of them contributed to the person you are and the life you live today.

Now, let's do an exercise that calls for a trip down memory lane and some introspection. It's going to be worth it, I promise.

Make a list of the ten biggest decisions that changed your life one way or another. Then delve a little deeper and make a list of ten small decisions that didn't seem like much at the time but did, nonetheless, have a significant impact on your life. Once the two lists are ready, start analyzing each memory/ decision and ask yourself the following questions for each point:

- What were the circumstances under which I made the decision?

- What were my reasons for making the decision that I did?

- Was I happy with my decision?

- Am I happy with its consequences?

- What would I have done differently?

- What would I repeat?

- If I were to make the decision once again, knowing what I know about its effects and life in general after that, would I still make the decision I did?

- Did I make the decision on my own or was I forced/ advised into it?

- What are the lessons the experience taught me?

- How do I feel about making decisions as a result?

Chapter 9

Decision-Making 101

Have you ever wondered why decision-making comes so easily to a select few but most of us tend to hem-and-haw when we are faced with having to take important decisions. Have you ever wondered why the ability to make decisions swiftly but thoughtfully is often associated with a courageous personality? Where does daring and nerve come into decision-making? Why is it so scary to make decisions?

Decision-making can be terrifying because it's nearly impossible to tell how the future is going to shape up and not knowing the results your decisions are going to have can be worrying. However, sometimes the only option you have is to plough on forward and have faith in yourself and your reasons for coming to the conclusion you have.

But even being able to do that involves some kind of strength, some skill. That's what we're going to learn here. Here are some techniques for making great decisions.

9.1 Know Your Info Threshold

Too little information and you might end up making the wrong decision, too much and it will leave you exhausted. You can never know exactly what the right amount of knowledge on any topic is but you can develop a sense for how much time and mind space you'd like to spend on an issue. Learn all you need to know but don't fatigue yourself trying to exhaust every resource.

9.2 Dialectical Bootstrapping

It's always advisable to seek multiple opinions and lots of advice, but what if you have to make a decision in a hurry or you generally don't have access to trusted council? Dialectical bootstrapping is technique by which you 'play' all the different sides and debate the pros and cons of every option-thereby evaluating your choices from multiple perspectives and not just an individual one. The more you practice being able to debate all the perspectives, the better you get at it.

9.3 Learn To Process Data

We've talked about needing information for making decisions, and about limiting how much we expose ourselves to. The thing is, there are three stages to facts about any situation/ option: data, information and finally, knowledge. Data by itself is just rough-hewn facts. Information is also data, albeit in a more processed form. And knowledge is information that has been refined such that you now have a lesson and understanding attached to the raw data. As far as possible, try to collect facts that are already at the final stage and when you can't, learn to process it all yourself as quickly as you can. The better you get at absorbing material, the faster you'll be able to make the most of it without having to expend too much of your energy.

Part 4

Taking Action & Producing Results

Once you become comfortable with leadership tasks like assuming responsibility and making decisive choices, the next step is to be able to actually act on those roles. Where responsibility and decision-making fall into the more cognitive aspects of your personality, the ability to move beyond thought and into action forms a more outwardly dynamic element of your being.

In this segment, we take a look at the importance of moving from thought to action and the perils of leading a passive life. We are also going to discuss techniques and strategies for actively pursuing your passions, dreams and plans and realizing them in all their potential.

So, in keeping with the theme, let's get moving!

Chapter 10

The Power Of Action & The Price Of Passivity

Have you ever wondered about the difference between actions, reactions and inaction? Ever thought about which you're most likely to resort to?

What we're essentially looking into is whether you have an assertive personality or a passive one. Leaders typically have assertive, take-charge personalities because they do not like to sit around and wait and watch while things unfold around them. If you are the kind of person who enjoys fixing and achieving goals and you don't believe in taking a chance on things that are important to you, you have an assertive personality. This means that it is not enough for you to want things; you act to manufacture your reality and don't wait for it to materialize.

A lot of people associate assertiveness with aggressiveness. As a result, people who do not like confrontation and have a more easygoing personality often choose to hold back and let things happen as they may. They want to avoid unpleasantness, and in a bid to do so, often get relegated to the sidelines of their own life. There is absolutely nothing wrong with enjoying peace and stability and wanting to avoid negativity; in fact, that is how everyone should be able to live. But the problem with being passive is that while it might help you avoid stress, antagonism and awkward situations, it is also going to cause you to miss out on life's opportunities. In other words, the path of least resistance might be free of bumps and craters, but it isn't exactly dressed with laurels and accomplishments either.

The basic problem with passivity is that it reduces you to a spectator in your own life. If that sounds harsh, just consider how unpleasant it is to never be able to get things to go according to your plans! If you aren't sure of your personality type just yet, ask yourself the following questions:

- Do you find yourself saying 'yes' to people's requests an demands when you just want to say 'no'?

- Do you constantly find yourself inconvenienced and at a disadvantage because you're doing something for someone else- yet again?

- Do you worry about hurting other people's feelings- and so you would rather just 'suck it up' and do what they want?

- Do you find it difficult to communicate your own hurt feelings?

- Are you constantly bottling up and biting back your own opinions- even when the topic at hand has the potential to impact you?

If you've answered in the affirmative to any of these questions, you have a passive personality. Remember how, in the very first chapter of this book, we talked about how the world is divided into actors and audiences: your personality type determines which category you fall into; are you a proactive lead in your life or a passive spectator?

Chapter 11

Make The Leap: From Dreamer To Doer

Have you ever wondered why everyone has big ideas, ambitions and dreams but only a handful of people actually manage to live them out?

Do you remember how back in your school or university days the entire group would talk about their professional ambitions and everyone seemed poised to be a superstar, but as you grew up there are just one or two people who've actually managed to make good on their plans?

Why does that happen? Why do some people become roaring successes- just as they said they would- while others fail to realize their dreams? It's not as though some dreams are worthier than others. The difference is simple, and heartbreaking:

most people are content with dreaming, so they never get around to acting on them. Or they're inhibited, scared of failing or otherwise discouraged.

But, as they say, if you never try you'll never know. And the astonishing, uplifting fact is that most of the time, when you try and you try hard, you actually succeed beyond your wildest dreams.

When it comes to achieving and accomplishing, the world is divided into two kinds of people: the dreamers and the doers. Before you jump the gun and argue that 'dreamers are important *also*', know this: dreamers dream, but they don't always do but doers usually dream *and* they do! How's that for a thought-provoking bit of alliterative inspiration?

You don't have to give up on your creative, visionary ways to be able to become proactive. Quite the contrary, actually: you need to focus on your dreams more so than ever before, but this time you need to also chart out action plans on how to take your dreams from thoughts and ideas in your mind to actually lived-out experiences in real time.

In this chapter, we're going to take a look at how you can learn to be proactive. The characteristic that defines proactive people is that they don't wait for things to happen and then react; they act ahead of time. In other words, while your 'response' might actually be the same whether you're being proactive or reactive, it's when you choose to affect it that makes all the difference. You're either taking an initiative or you're tackling the situation when there's no way left around it.

As we've discussed, a passive personality might make for a generally harmonious atmosphere but it does restrict you from pursuing your goals and dreams. So, if you want to lead- in business, in society, in life- you have to focus on retaining the pleasant aspects of your personality while doing away with those that hold you back.

How, you might ask? Let's look at some habits of leaders that you can incorporate starting today.

11.1 Action Strategies Of The Aces- BE The Leader!

11.1.1 Get Moving Right Away

Start planning the moment you notice something that needs acting on. You will be surprised to see just how much time is required to be able to analyze a situation, isolate options, weigh possibilities, take a decision, make a plan and *then* get to the action part. You can't just identify a need or a trigger and instantaneously jump to action; you need to be able to move through all the necessary stages at the right pace and in the correct order. Doing so involves time and energy. If you put off beginning until a later time, you'll never get around to meeting your targets in the desired timeframes.

11.1.2 Don't Wait On Others

As a leader you probably have an entire team of people working under you as well as counterparts working with you. It can be tempting to 'wait till everyone's ready' or you might even feel like it's the most democratic thing to do. However, if you actually start waiting on people to do the things you need to do, you'll be waiting forever. Remember this, nobody else can lead *for* you. People might help you, support you and nurture you but they can't play your role for you. It's all down to you.

11.1.3 Consistency Of Action

You might be feeling revved up from all this talk about taking charge and taking action and doing stuff, but know that there's a difference between being active and being erratic. You don't want to suddenly start running amok all over the place, affecting changes that aren't conducive to your vision or your team. You don't want to start taking action just for the sake of it. You must act to keep moving ahead, not to keep running around in the same spot. You must be consistent and stable and have a proper strategy in place. Let there be some meaning to your actions, some need that rationalizes them.

11.1.4 Surround Yourself With Driven People

The company you keep has a significant impact on your success rate. You can find motivation in your team, family and friends or you can get turned away from your goals. The people around us- even if they're not actively trying to sway us- are some of the most potent influencers in our lives. Have you ever noticed how successful people can always be found in the company of equally successful people?

It's a matter of like *choosing* like. If your company is complacent, lazy and apathetic, you'll lose your steam and enthusiasm too, soon enough. But if you want to maintain and magnify your momentum, you need to start seeking out people who are just as driven and dynamic as you are, if not more so.

Start acting on your plans today. I think Walt Disney said it most beautifully when he opined, "If you can dream it, you can do it".

Part 5

Taking On The World

In the previous segments of this e-book guide, you've learned to:

- Take stock of yourself to develop yourself into the individual and leader you want to be.

- Take responsibilities that empower others and enable you to work efficiently.

- Take decisions that help you move closer to your goals.

- And take actions that make your goals realities.

In this chapter, we look at the final aspects of crystallizing your identity and strengths as a leader.

The coming chapters will help you put the finishing touches on your role as a leader. We're going to help you realize your specific leadership style and share some great techniques on how to become an even more proficient leader than you already are.

Now it is finally time to emerge as the leader you have always been meant to be, and take on the world!

Chapter 12

RaDaR-The Interlink

Have you ever wondered why the people who do one thing right usually manage to do everything right? They know what needs to be done, they plan well for it, they act on their preparations efficiently, they get the results they seek and they always come out on top, no matter what.

We all know that one person who has a great job, a great education, a fantastic house, a fulfilling relationship, a happy family, a clean bill of health and every happiness that money can and can't buy. Most of the time we resort to phrases like, "oh, he/she is so lucky" or "why does he/she have everything but I don't have anything?" or even, "it's so unfair, why don't my dreams come true?"

The problem with thinking like this is twofold:

- You're being fatalistic and probably aren't being honest with yourself about the fact that you haven't worked to earn the things you want.

- You're undermining someone else's hard work and spirit and dismissing their achievements by calling it a result of 'good luck' and not recognizing the labor that's gone into it.

In this book, the entire crux of all our leadership lessons has been the fact that your plans won't work if you don't. If you want your dreams to come true you need to ask yourself, "what did I do today that will help me move closer to achieving my goals?"

When you're pouring over that old high school rival's vacation photos on Facebook or gossiping with a colleague about another coworker who's got a fabulous apartment, dive a little deeper and you'll see that those who constantly enjoy good luck are the ones that make their own luck. If you want to be lucky all you need to do is start targeting the three elements of success that we've discussed in this book: responsibilities, decisions and actions. These three fundamentals are at the heart of any plan and how you leverage them will completely determine your successes or failures.

You might question, is any one of these elements more powerful than the others? It's human nature to be inquisitive and to want adapt things, but when it comes to becoming successful in life, the answer is no: you need to be responsible, you need to make choices and you need to act, all in equal measure and while moving seamlessly from one stage to the other.

While the willingness and skill to take on responsibilities and make decisions is indispensable to being a leader, so is the ability to take action. You can't argue that one is more important than the other: after all, what is the point of thinking things through and forming decisions if they don't translate from your mind and words into reality? Likewise, you can't really run around planning and doing things without putting in the necessary amount of thought, appraisal and consideration into them.

Chapter 13

Living The Leader's Life

Have you ever wondered why people we like to call 'natural-born leaders' seem to radiate a certain magnetism throughout the day, and not just at work? It's not because they're "born leaders" but because they understand a powerful secret: leadership is a lifestyle and a way of being, not just something that you switch on when you step into your workplace.

Good leaders are leaders in every sphere of life: work, home, family, society, money matters, politics etc. They're opinion-makers, gatekeepers and game-changers. They don't take turns at being leaders versus not. Leadership is not something you can take days off from. And while it's certainly a lot of hard work and responsibility, if you do it right it's not something exhausting that you should want rest breaks from.

Once you decide to be a leader, you've got to start living the leader's life. Here are some sensational skills for becoming a life leader.

13.1 Set Examples

Ever heard of leading by example? Show people the best way to do something by doing it yourself. Whether you want your employees to use energy resources judiciously or you want to teach your toddler the value of sharing, the most effective way of inducing a change is to be someone others want to emulate.

All of us have heroes and role models that we idolize. Do you know how that works? When we look up to someone we want to be more like him or her. We want to be worthy of the same kind of respect and admiration that they inspire in us. And so we set about changing our ways and adapting our habits to reflect theirs. From that one teacher in high school who had the power of inspiring you beyond the textbooks to your next-door-neighbor who taught you about kindness and selflessness, I'm very sure you have people you remember looking up to till this very day. And if people have inspired you to be more and do more by simply pursuing higher ideals themselves, shouldn't you do the same as a leader?

Making rules for people is easy, and it works, but it's not true leadership. True, lasting leadership penetrates deep into people's psyche and makes them want to change on their own. When you set a strong example, you get the behavior you're looking for without having to ask for it.

13.2 Master Communication

All our experiences would be meaningless if we couldn't communicate: how else do you share ideas, opinions, plans, advice, strategies and feelings? You can argue that faulty communication is better than no communication, but it can do a lot of damage! As a leader you need to be able to succinctly deliver all your visions to people in the clearest, most precise form at all times.

Learn to keep communication short, simple, to the point, respectful and goal-oriented. Pay attention to body language and non-verbal clues, both your own and other people's.

Communication is key to:

- Getting things done
- Isolating problems, mistakes and wrongful patterns

- Correcting mistakes

- Sharing experiences

- Sharing knowledge

- Working together

- The human experience

Proper effective communication ensures that the message the sender is giving out is exactly the one that is understood by the recipient, in the shortest amount of time possible. Effective communication decreases misunderstandings, wasted time and wasted energy.

13.3 Learn To Represent

Most of your days as a leader will be spent on teaching people skills, working towards goals and assessing priorities. That's how you keep moving ahead in life. However, every now and then you will need to step out of that space and act as the face of the team you represent. This could be your organization, a brand, a movement, your family or your community. Learning to represent properly and powerfully is an indispensable life skill. And a very important one at that, because your success with this skill decides how people view you and also what they think of the people/ cause you represent. When you're playing a representative role, whether it is in a public or interpersonal setting, you must always be on your best behavior, be mindful of why you're here, remember what you hope to achieve from this exercise and never lose sight of your role as the ambassador of something that extends beyond you. It's both a symbolic and dynamic responsibility.

13.4 Praise, Credit And Acknowledge Others

All of us like to be showered with affection and approval, and when we've worked hard for something it means even more than usual. If you like people to look up to you for your successes and efforts, just imagine how much it must mean to the people looking up to you to have you appreciate the role they've played in all of it. No single person in an endeavor is ever more deserving than all the rest; even when you're a leader you're a part of a team and that team deserves as much acknowledgment as you do. Identify people's strengths, applaud them, commend their good work and be generous (and genuine) with the compliments. Whether you're appreciating your spouse for picking up the chores or employees for meeting a target, always give credit where it's due.

Chapter 14

Develop Your Leadership Style

Have you ever wondered why some people always know what to do, no matter what the situation at hand is? They know what the right thing to say to a person is, they know what the right response to a trigger is, they know what the right choice in a tricky spot is and they always know how to convince people to see things their way. They just seem to know the secret to doing and being right. It's like they just can't go wrong.

Do you want to know what that secret is? They know their leadership style. They know who they are as a leader, and how they like to lead. And so, even if the situations, dynamics, names, faces and stakes keep changing, they have an insight into how they'd like to react. This knowledge shapes their choices. It makes them ready for anything.

Confused? Think of it as a blueprint for life decisions. How do patterns and characteristics help us? They define us. And when they define us, they let us in on preferences and techniques and strengths and weaknesses. You know how practice makes us perfect? Well, once you identify your leadership style you can keep practicing it until it becomes second nature to you. This way, every single time that you are faced with a choice or a decision you don't need to return to the drawing board and carve out a new solution: you already know who you are and the kind of results you would like to see and the distances between these two values will inform you of the choices you need to make.

14.1 Different Leadership Styles: Which One Are You?

There are five main kinds of leadership styles. The way I see it, your innate qualities can define the leadership style you naturally gravitate towards or, and here's where being in control and taking action comes into play, you can evaluate the different styles and choose the one you like the most and believe will be most beneficial to everyone involved.

14.1.1 Authoritarian Leadership

The autocratic leader is firm and works with a tight fist.

The difference between the leader and the followers is strictly established and maintained.

The leader gives orders, monitors effort and progress and corrects shortcomings.

Followers are not invited to contribute to the decision-making process, and are simply tasked with completing their duties as per the leader's instructions. Most experts are of the opinion that with this kind of leadership, when things get done it is mostly because of a fear of negative repercussions and punishment. As such, it is not a very healthy or happy atmosphere to function in.

Communication generally follows a top-down, unidirectional route.

14.1.2 Democratic Leadership

This is, by far, the most all-inclusive form of leadership that there is.

In this kind of leadership the leader works *with* the people and they don't work *for* the leader. Everyone works for the goal or the cause, however it may be defined.

The responsibility of meeting targets and the success of doing so are shared by everyone- including the leader.

Communication exists at and between all levels of the hierarchy and moves both horizontally and vertically. Such leaders generally maintain an 'open door policy' and issue a permanent invitation to everyone to seek them out whenever needed.

Democratic leaders are counselors and advisors: they help the team in all their efforts, from identifying lacunae in existing systems to coming up with creative solutions to problems.

It is important to note that even though this kind of leadership is marked by equal investment and participation on the part of everyone, the leader is still clearly recognized and respected for his or her role.

14.1.3 Laissez-fair Leadership

In this kind of leadership the leader accords complete responsibility and decision-making authority to their followers. It's a laid back form of leadership because the entire onus of goal accomplishment and even goal-setting falls completely upon the team.

Critics state that in such situations the leader is little more than a figurehead. The leader doesn't have a hands-on approach and as such doesn't do any 'leading' at all.

In a lot of these cases if the leader is too lenient or uninvolved most tasks will remain unfulfilled and the organization will usually fritter away.

However, the flip side is that if the leader is able to inspire the team enough and be present just enough, the team may develop into an extremely independent, skilled and productive one.

If you want to cull out unproductive team members and gather together a team of highly specialized people without having to actively participate in goal achievement yourself, it is important to learn to walk the line between being too involved and being missing too often.

It is recommended that this kind of leadership should be supplemented with external evaluations, monitoring and consultation. Getting a third-party to sit in on a frequent basis can help bridge the gap between the leader and the team without needing either party to take time out from their other pursuits.

14.1.4 Transactional Leadership

This kind of leadership is based on the carrots-and-sticks principle: desirable behavior is celebrated while undesirable behavior is penalized. This way, followers want to earn more rewards and avoid punishment, and so they alter their actions to be able to do the same.

The rewards and punishments can be both tangible and psychological, from a change in salaries and positions and material compensation to a change in the interpersonal dynamic and group recognition for good/ bad behavior.

In this kind of leadership, the leader cements their position by doling out praise vs. punishment and the followers' prerogative is to keep moving towards goal accomplishment.

Followers are not expected to challenge or change the status quo in any manner, and they are not likely to want that either.

Transactional leadership is generally not concerned with charting new routes to achieving aims, but with improving existing practices to be able to do so. The point is to augment the good and eliminate the bad without bringing in an entirely new system into action.

14.1.5 Transformational Leadership

This type of leadership involves *transforming* other people's views, beliefs and habits so that they may move closer to goal achievement. As such, it relies on an inspirational and motivational factor where people are stirred into action.

Transformational leaders are usually very charismatic and have two weapons in their arsenal:

- An attractive personality that draws people towards them.

- First-hand, field experience with the tasks and niches they aim to lead others through. This gives them legitimacy and credibility, and these can go a long way in making people want to follow you.

A defining feature of transformational leadership is that the leader gives personalized, dedicated attention to every member of the team. Since the point is to be able to get people to change from within, the leader must familiarize himself or herself with each person's strengths, weaknesses, habits, ambitions and roles. Everybody functions in a unique way and we all need different triggers and incentives to want to change. In other words, the leader needs to know what makes each person tick. The transformational leader believes in individualizing his or her efforts to suit every single person.

It goes without saying that the kind of leadership style you follow will affect the atmosphere in your surroundings. Your choice might be influenced by the industry or setting, but it should ideally based on your objectives, the welfare of the people you lead and the kind of leader you want to be remembered as.

14.2 Leadership Fundamentals

Now, whichever leadership category you fall into- or even if you develop your own style- there are certain basic habits and strategies that you should practice. Doing so will make it easier for you to enact your choices as a leader, and will also set the tone for the kind of atmosphere you want around yourself. The practices that we are going to discuss now apply regardless of industry, age, context and goal; these are just a few neat little tricks that can help you consolidate your approach to leadership a little faster.

14.2.1 Don't Justify, Explain

One of the biggest challenges when you're making the leap from passivity to leadership is that you'll often find yourself slipping into familiar patterns and wanting to make things easier for others. Remember, a leader cares for the people around him or her but also respects their own role first. You might want to explain your actions and decisions, but don't justify them. This makes you look and feel weak and you'll only second-guess yourself. If you aren't sure of your decisions you cannot expect others to follow your path. When you do arrive at a decision, have confidence in your reasons and share the same with others.

14.2.2 Blend Team And Goal Management

When you start assuming your position as a leader, there are three things you must do as far as your team is concerned:

- Practice the utmost clarity in explaining expectations, roles, tasks, and duties.

- Encourage, accept and incorporate feedback.

- Enforce rules without fail. You've worked hard on your plan. Stick to it. Make sure everyone else does too. You need to be understanding and accommodating when the situation calls for it, but nothing should ever take away from the end goal. Everyone must deliver as is expected of them.

14.2.3 Empower Others

If you look at the people working with you (whether they're working alongside you or under you) as competition, you are never going to make it far as a leader. Yes, you have competitors and you need to identify them and work to get ahead of them- within ethical limits, of course. But the people who constitute your team are not your competition. Leaders who start setting team members against each other or consciously try to curtail their team members and limit their potential and successes are not leaders at all. They're opportunists. And you cannot go very far if you aren't genuinely interested in helping your team go far as well. Look at it this way: ever goal accomplish is both an individual victory and a collective triumph. And leaders recognize that they are only as good as their teams and they appreciate and celebrate each individual's contribution to success.

Make it a point to empower the people you surround yourself with, in any way possible. You could help them recognize and isolate their strengths and weaknesses and suggest strategies for managing and enhancing as is needed. You can provide suggestions and feedback on ongoing projects to help fine-tune the same. You should always maintain open channels of communication and invite (and uphold) everyone's confidence so that they can seek out your guidance as and when they need it.

Being a leader is all about proactively offering people a helping hand. And any time you feel tempted not to, whatever your reasons, remember that you've made it this far because of people who helped you along. You should pay it forward!

14.2.4 Fake It Till You Make It

To some people leadership comes naturally, while others have to cultivate it. If you are one of the latter and you are using this book to find your footing, remember that everyone starts out somewhere. So it is okay if you feel unsure of yourself sometimes.

Leadership can be exhilarating, but can also take a while to get used to. Do remember though, while you get used to your new self, just be sure to project comfort and confidence. People will believe what you show them. So if you're trying to take control but expressing your frustration and uncertainty that is what they are going to respond to. But if you act comfortable and at-ease with your role as a powerful individual, they are going to feel safe following you.

Play the part in the early days by emulating other leaders you look up to and using the strategies discussed in this book. One day you will wake up and realize that you no longer need to make a conscious effort at being a leader because somewhere along the way you've already become one!

Conclusion

You've come this far and should be very proud of yourself. It doesn't take much to want to be something, but it takes a lot to decide to be it and then act on it. The fact that you've pursued the book till the very end is by itself a mark of your dedication.

But a leader's work is never over, and the best leaders are the ones that continuously keep learning, growing and evolving. Now all you need to do is keep up the commitment and start acting on the lessons that you have learned here.

It's easy to blame our circumstances on social demands, familial issues, bad habits, peer pressure, limited means, lack of opportunity and so on but remember what we discussed earlier in this guide about how you have to make your own luck? I must reiterate the importance of getting up and going after what you want because that's the only way you will ever get it!

The single most powerful strength, inhibitor, enabler and influencer in your successes, or the lack of them, is YOU!

What you do or don't do has a greater impact than all the other factors put together.

Yes, it takes a little while to get used to the fact that you are not a victim of your circumstances, especially since it involves admitting your own flaws and complacency. But once you've crossed that uncomfortable threshold, there is nothing to hold you back. That was the old you and this is the new you. And the new you is ready to lead the world!

I hope this guide has been helpful to you in realizing and molding your potential as a leader. Leadership extends to every part of life, and once you start using the strategies and advice described in this book you will see that you start enjoying success, joy and contentment in just about every sphere of your life.

If you benefit from the book- and I'm sure you will- be sure to recommend it to others and empower them on their journey forward.

www.ingramcontent.com/pod-product-compliance
Lightning Source LLC
Chambersburg PA
CBHW072158090426
42740CB00012B/2312